"High in the trees overhead he heard a thin singing . . ."

SAILING to CYTHERA

AND OTHER ANATOLE STORIES

BY NANCY WILLARD

ILLUSTRATIONS BY DAVID MC PHAIL

HARCOURT BRACE JOVANOVICH

NEW YORK AND LONDON

Printed in the United States of America

First edition

B C D E F G H I J

Library of Congress Cataloging in Publication Data
Willard, Nancy.
Sailing to Cythera, and other Anatole stories.
CONTENTS: Gospel train.—The wise soldier of Sellebak.—Sailing to Cythera.
[1. Short stories] I. McPhail, David M., illus. II. Title.
PZ7.W6553Sai   [Fic]   74-5602
ISBN 0-15-269960-0

For James Anatole Lindbloom

CONTENTS

SAILING TO CYTHERA

GOSPEL TRAIN

here was once a boy who lived with a cat. The boy was called Anatole. The cat was called Plumpet, which tells you something about her size and habits. She was fond of field mice, herring, and whipped cream, and she had stripes the color of milk and honey.

In the summer Anatole lived at Plumpet's cottage behind the woodshed. Afternoons they would sit outside under the apple tree while Plumpet knitted and Anatole played with his train and sang:

> "The Gospel Train is coming.
> I hear it just at hand,
> I hear those wheels a-rumbling
> and rolling through the land."

His papa had taught him that song and had given him, for his fifth birthday, a gold pocket watch with an engine engraved on the back. It had belonged to Anatole's grand-papa who was once a train conductor. The hands on the watch always said a quarter of eleven, regardless of what other clocks said.

Sometimes his papa took him to the train station to watch the trains come in and out. Once the engineer of the Penn Central's nine-thirty to New York had let them ride as far as the end of the platform.

Anatole always invited Plumpet to come, too, but she refused. And she was not impressed with his American Flyer baggage car and two passenger cars, his Lionel engine and tender, his Babe Ruth boxcar, and his Chesapeake & Ohio gondola.

"What do I care about diesels and bells and water pumps?" she exclaimed. "What has all that to do with me?"

In the winter Plumpet moved into Anatole's house as there was no heat in her cottage. Other people lived in Anatole's house, too, but they are not in this story.

One spring morning Anatole woke up early and looked out of his window and saw Plumpet under the apple tree digging a hole with a silver spade. Generally she dug with her claws. Beside her stood a black cat holding a golden box, and as Plumpet dug, the black cat sang:

"Requiem eternam dona eis,
Lux perpetua luceat eis."

Then the black cat lowered the box into the hole, and Plumpet filled in the hole, and the black cat bowed, shouldered the spade, walked into the honeysuckle thicket, and was gone.

Anatole hurried outside, but Plumpet had gone around to the front yard and taken a tiny stone in her paws and was crouched in a patch of mint, drawing on the sidewalk that led past the garden to the street.

Her drawing looked like this:

"Is it for Hopscotch?" asked Anatole.

"Not Hopscotch," said the cat.

"Tiddlywinks?" asked Anatole.

"Not Tiddlywinks, either," said the cat.

"Hop-o'-my-Thumb."

"Not Hop-o'-my-Thumb."

"What then?" asked Anatole. "And what did you bury under the apple tree?"

Plumpet drew the last rung on her ladder.

"You remember my old Aunt Pitterpat, who lived in Roscoe's General Store," said Plumpet.

Anatole remembered a black-and-white cat nestled in the sunny window among the cigar boxes. Mrs. Roscoe always had black-and-white cats.

"I remember," he said.

"My Aunt Pitterpat has gone to get a new skin. She sent me the old one to bury, and she's invited us both to her christening party," said Plumpet. "Cats have nine lives and nine christenings. This is Pitterpat's ninth. I've drawn a railroad track, so the train can find us."

And Plumpet scratched a tiny hole under the peonies and buried her writing stone.

"No trains run on Grand Avenue," said Anatole. "And we're miles away from the station."

"All things come to those who wait," said Plumpet, and she sat down on a bench that was not there until she looked for it.

A man hurried past them, pushing a baggage cart, and then a train whistle sounded, far beyond the garden. The flowers closed their petals and dreamed of a train platform, on which Anatole now found himself standing, much to his surprise, watching the train rush closer and closer.

"You see," said Plumpet, "doubt is the root of all failure."

It was as comfortable a train as you could wish for. There was a first-class coach, with doors that locked if you wished to sit alone. There was a coach for eating supper, and a coach for playing checkers, and a coach for drinking tea, and a sleeping coach.

Plumpet and Anatole rode in the second-class coach. Across the aisle sat two owls in bonnets. In the seat opposite Anatole, a raccoon was reading the newspaper. Behind them, a mouse child's voice squeaked, "Is that Grainesville, Mother?"

"*Across the aisle sat two owls in bonnets. In the seat opposite
Anatole, a raccoon was reading the newspaper.*"

"Not yet," said a deeper voice. "Soon."

The conductor, a handsome Barbary sheep, did not collect tickets. Instead, he walked up and down the aisle and called out the stops.

"Pudding Street Station! Pumpkin Lane next!"

And late in the afternoon he called out, "St. John's Meadow! Fifteen-minute stop for anyone wishing to pick a bouquet!"

When the train stopped at St. John's Meadow, everyone got off. The air was warm and sweet. Far away at the edge of the meadow, Anatole saw a family of rabbits cutting hay and spreading it on racks to dry and singing as they worked:

> "O, the racing of the sun
> and the rising of the moon.
> These flowers green and tall
> must go the way of all,
> and winter comes too soon.
>
> "O, the sparrows in the sky
> and the dragons in the sea.
> In mad or merry weather,
> we'll take our rest together
> under the apple tree."

Anatole remembered his apple tree at home, and he was so happy that he didn't feel like picking anything. Instead, he walked to the front of the train and investigated the engine. A fox in a jaunty blue cap sat in the engineer's seat. A squirrel was shoveling coal into the firebox.

"This is an old train," said Anatole to himself. "Nowadays, they have diesel engines."

Plumpet picked some catnip, and the raccoon stuck a primrose into his lapel. He offered one to Plumpet, who refused, saying she did not affect clothes.

"All aboard," called the conductor.

When the train started up, everyone took out picnic hampers and lunch boxes except the raccoon, who took out a cigar.

"Ah, dear." Plumpet sighed. "We've forgotten to pack a lunch."

The two owls, seeing their predicament, offered them three roasted mice and a small bottle of elderberry wine. Anatole could not bring himself to eat the mice, but he found the elderberry wine very good, and he drank his share quickly. Plumpet never ate or drank anything quickly. She said it harmed the digestion. She ate the mice slowly between loud purrs.

"Lovely plump little things," she said, licking her chin. And she gazed wickedly across the aisle.

"I hope you're not thinking of eating the owls," exclaimed Anatole.

"Certainly not," said Plumpet, shocked. "It's against the rules here. Where would we all be if we tried to eat each other up?"

Suddenly the coach grew dark. A hen roosting on the baggage rack tucked her head under her wing. Anatole looked out the window. The train was entering a thick forest, where presently it stopped.

"This is the border," said Plumpet. "This is where the ferryman collects his toll and carries us across the river."

"You mean the train goes on a boat?" asked Anatole, very much interested.

Plumpet yawned. "How should I know? What does it matter so long as we get there?"

The train started up again, and now water lapped on both sides of them. But before Anatole could tell how the crossing was done, they had reached the other side and entered a tunnel carved into an enormous tree.

"This is the gate to Morgentown," said Plumpet. "I should love to have a postcard of it to hang in my cottage. But nobody in Morgentown sends postcards."

When they arrived, it was twilight. ("It's never night in Morgentown," the conductor assured them.) Lanterns twinkled like low stars over the city square. Cats jostled past them on bicycles, and rabbits pulled carts piled high with cabbages, and falcons hawked pieces of sky, souvenirs of Morgentown.

"A fake," said the raccoon. "The sky sailed out of reach years ago. Good-bye."

"How shall we find your Aunt Pitterpat?" asked Anatole. It did not seem possible to find anyone here among so many. Plumpet was not discouraged.

"She sent me word to look for her at the party. She's probably riding the merry-go-round. Oh, Pitterpat was always a great one for rides. She used to jump into Mrs. Roscoe's car every chance she got."

When they came to the merry-go-round, there was Pitterpat perched on a white horse moving up and down, up and down to the music.

"Climb aboard!" she called. "This ride never stops, and the music goes on forever."

So Anatole grabbed a red horse and Plumpet leaped on a blue one, and Pitterpat rode between them.

"You're looking well," observed Plumpet. "Your new skin is the same color as your old one."

"Yes, and it won't wear out. The ninth skin lasts forever."

"Shall you be coming back to the store?" asked Anatole.

"No," said Pitterpat sadly. "Give my love to my kittens, Plumpet. Has Mrs. Roscoe found good homes for them yet?"

"I think," said Plumpet, "she's going to keep them herself."

"Ah," said Pitterpat, "I'd like to give them a little treat, but we aren't allowed to send anything out of here. But tell them I'm happy." Her voice sounded sad, but behind the sadness she was purring. "And enjoy yourselves. Don't drink too much blackberry juice. It will make you so sleepy that you'll miss the train home."

"If we miss the first train, we'll catch the next one," said Plumpet.

But Pitterpat looked grave.

"If you miss the midnight special, you'll never be able to leave. That's in the rules for visitors. If you miss the train, you must stay here forever."

"We'll be careful," said Anatole.

"One last thing," said Pitterpat. "The kittens are so fond of catnip. Do you think, Plumpet, you could plant them a little bush—"

"Don't mention it," said Plumpet.

"Enjoy yourselves," said Pitterpat.

And they did enjoy themselves. They rode the merry-go-round and the Ferris wheel, and then they went back to the merry-go-round, and then Plumpet said, "I'm starved."

"Look, there's a cafe," said Anatole. "Wouldn't it be fun to eat under one of those purple umbrellas?"

While they were sipping their blackberry juice and eating their chocolate ice cream, Anatole spied a train running round and round on a little track.

"Oh, Plumpet," he exclaimed. "Let's ride on that!"

"What? Why, we've bounced about in a train half the day, and you're ready to ride another one! Well, I can't let you ride it alone."

But she enjoyed herself all the same.

When the lanterns fell asleep and the sun came up, a pig in a long blue coat crossed the square, ringing a bell and shouting, "Last train out! All those leaving for the mainland, last train out!"

"Oh!" exclaimed Anatole. "I forgot all about the time!"

And with Plumpet at his heels, he hurried away from the party.

They boarded the train, and the conductor pulled up the stairs after them. The cars were nearly full. Plumpet and Anatole took the last seats. Then they waited for the train to move.

They waited and waited. Anatole took out his watch

and studied it. The hands said a quarter of eleven, of course.

"What can be the matter?" exclaimed the raccoon.

And a turtle said, "I need not have hurried. That's clear."

At last the conductor entered the car.

"I have bad news for all of you," he announced. "Our engineer has not returned. The truth is, I fear he drank too much blackberry juice and has fallen asleep under a hedge somewhere. Does anyone in this car know how to drive a train?"

And he glanced anxiously around him. Not a paw went up.

"Do you mean to say that we can't get out of here?" demanded the raccoon.

Then Anatole raised his hand. "I know something about trains. I believe I could drive it if the squirrel would help me."

"I suppose I had better come, too," said Plumpet, "in case a pair of stout claws is needed."

The squirrel was only too happy to help. He threw a shovel of coal on the fire. Anatole opened the throttle and Plumpet pulled the whistle cord. Slowly the train began to move through the enormous tree, out of the city.

"Do any other trains use this track?" asked Anatole.

"Nobody uses this track but us," said the squirrel.

"Good," said Anatole. And Plumpet curled up by the firebox for a nap.

As the train entered the woods, thunder exploded close by and lightning danced on the tracks. Plumpet woke up in alarm.

"There's the river ahead of us," shouted the squirrel, "but where's the bridge? Stop the train!"

Hastily Anatole closed the throttle.

"I thought the train crossed the river by boat," said Anatole. "But I don't see a boat. How did the fox do it?"

"I don't know," said the squirrel crossly. "I pay attention to my own job. How should I know what the fox did?"

The train chugged to a stop.

"Excuse me," said Anatole, standing up.

"I'm coming with you," said Plumpet.

Anatole walked through the cars until he found the two owls in bonnets. Of all the creatures on the train, they alone were wide awake.

"Ladies," he said, "I know it's very wet outside, but I need someone who can fly and who can see in the dark. Somewhere there's a boat that will take us across the river, and I can't find it."

The owls took their bonnets and folded them carefully on the seat.

"Open the window," chirped the big owl.

"Lend us a paw," said Plumpet. And she bit the Barbary sheep very gently on the neck and the raccoon very gently on the tail. They woke up at once.

"Together, now, push!" shouted Anatole.

The Barbary sheep and the raccoon and the cat and Anatole all pushed. The window flew open, and the rain rushed in, and the birds flew out.

"Close the window!" cackled the hen on the baggage rack.

"What's the matter?" asked a rabbit, rubbing his eyes.

"We're stuck," said Plumpet. "Nothing to worry about."

All over the car, animals woke and looked about them in bewilderment. Anatole pressed his nose to the window. Suddenly he saw two pale shapes fluttering outside.

"There they are! Push!"

The window flew up, and the owls flew in.

"Achoo," sneezed the small owl. "We saw a hundred white lions."

"God bless you," exclaimed the turtle. "Lions!"

"An old man was sitting with them," added the big owl.

"Somebody must go and ask him for help," said the raccoon.

"I'll go," said Anatole. "After all, I'm the engineer."

"We'll both go," announced Plumpet. "Open the door. In such weather I'm glad I do not wear clothes that wrinkle and muss."

The Barbary sheep and the turtle opened the door, and the boy and the cat stepped out.

Suddenly the rain stopped. Ahead of them, the river eddied white in the moonlight. On the bank lay the lions, their heads on their paws, and in their midst sat an old fisherman dressed in a sheepskin coat.

"He looks like a thistle," whispered Plumpet. "White hair, white beard, white coat, white boots. I think he fell into a flour barrel."

"Please, sir," called Anatole.

The lions rumbled and lifted their heads.

"Who are you?" roared the old man.

"I am Anatole. I am driving the train to the mainland, and I want to cross the river. Where's the boat?"

"This is my river, and my lions are the boat," said the old man. "What will you pay me for taking you across?"

"What do you want?" asked Anatole.

"The fox always gives me a piece of the sky."

Anatole shook his head. "But I don't have such a thing."

"Maybe you have a piece hidden in your pockets?" asked the old man.

Anatole turned his pockets inside out. "All I have is this watch."

The old man seized the watch. "How marvelous! A watch from the world where people still keep time!"

"It doesn't run," said Anatole. "Purely sentimental value. Please give it back."

The old man whistled a little tune. Then he said, "If you want me to carry your train across the river, give me the watch."

Silently Anatole handed him the watch.

Then the old man glanced down at Anatole's shoes. "How marvelous! Shoes from the world where things still wear out!"

"My sneakers? They're all raggedy," said Anatole nervously. "And the laces are broken."

The old man whistled a little tune. Then he said, "If you want me to carry your train across the river, give me your shoes."

So Anatole took off his shoes and gave them to the old man, who took off his white boots and put on the

"Silently Anatole handed him the watch."

sneakers. Much to Anatole's surprise, they fitted him.

Then the old man glanced up at Anatole's shirt and sighed. "What a wonderful shirt! What is that inscription on it?"

"My T-shirt? It says *Oxford, Michigan, Gravel Capital of the World*. I got it when I went to visit my grandma."

"Your grandma lives in a gravel pit?" inquired the old man.

"No," said Anatole. "She lives in Oxford. Most everyone around there works at the pit."

"How marvelous!" exclaimed the old man. "A shirt from the world where people still go to work every morning!"

"It's very dirty," said Anatole. "You should see the collar."

The old man whistled a little tune. Then he said, "If you want me to carry your train across the river, give me your shirt."

So Anatole took off his T-shirt and gave it to the old man, who took off his sheepskin coat and put on the shirt. Much to Anatole's surprise, it fitted him.

Then the old man said, "I've taken your clothes. You shall have mine. Now drive your train down to the river. I will command my lions to form a raft with their bodies. Drive your train over their backs. My lions are very strong. And I will stand at the front of the raft and pole you across."

The old man walked among his lions and called them down to the water. Anatole put on the old man's boots and coat.

"Very handsome," said Plumpet. "Let's go."

But Anatole could not move. His feet seemed glued to the earth.

"I can't," he said. "These clothes are too heavy."

"What a shame!" clucked Plumpet. "Isn't there some way of carrying them?"

Anatole kicked off the boots and pulled off the coat.

"It's no use. We'd better hurry. We're still a long way from home."

And he climbed aboard the train.

The hen on the baggage rack cocked her head at him.

"You've shed your clothes," she observed. "Are you moulting?"

"No," said Anatole. "Plumpet, tell everyone in the cars we're on our way."

The train rolled forward. Pressed close together, the lions formed a fine raft. At the head of them stood the old man, pushing the raft with a pole. And so smoothly did he dip the pole in and out that no one felt the train roll onto the opposite bank. When Anatole stuck his head out of the window, the lions looked like so many white boulders scattered in the river and the old man was nowhere to be seen. Ahead of them stretched a clearing—how different St. John's Meadow looked at night!

Then they came to a town, and then another town. One by one the animals got off.

Suddenly Anatole smelled something he loved, the apple trees and the mint in his mother's garden at home.

"Plumpet, wake up. This is our stop."

"Thank you for your help," said the squirrel, and he

jumped up on the engineer's seat. "We wouldn't have made it without you."

Anatole and Plumpet stood in the middle of the garden, in the middle of the night. The train was gone.

"You're a hero," said Plumpet.

"I don't feel like a hero. I'm sleepy," said Anatole.

"Go to bed then. I'm going out mousing for an hour or two. And I have promises to keep in the morning."

And that's why the next morning Anatole found himself looking out of his window at Plumpet, who was digging under the apple tree. With her claws she dug a little hole, and in the hole she planted the sprig of catnip she'd picked in St. John's Meadow. And as she planted, she sang lustily for anyone who cared to listen:

> "O, the racing of the sun
> and the rising of the moon.
> These flowers green and tall
> must go the way of all,
> and winter comes too soon.
>
> "O, the sparrows in the sky,
> and the dragons in the sea.
> In mad or merry weather,
> we'll take our rest together
> under the apple tree."

THE WISE SOLDIER
OF SELLEBAK

nder the apple tree Anatole stopped swinging. There, on a garbage pail in the alley, sat a tall blond man in a tattered blue uniform, eating an apple and cocking his head to hear Anatole's mother as she practiced "Awake, Ye Wintry Earth" in an uncertain alto for the Sunday service.

So of course Anatole walked right up to the garbage pail and waited for the man to speak.

But the stranger went right on eating his apple.

"Who are you?" demanded Anatole.

The stranger shook his head. "Don't know. Woke up this morning to find I'd been robbed of everything I had. Name, address, destination."

Anatole was so surprised that for a moment he could think of nothing to say. Still, he wanted to help.

"Did you check your pockets?" he inquired.

"What do you know about that!" The man slapped his knee. "Forgot to check my pockets."

He rummaged through his pockets and pulled out a large tooth.

"It once belonged to a reindeer," he said. "I carry it for luck."

As soon as he saw the tooth, Anatole wanted to trade his rabbit's foot for it, but the stranger was already tucking it carefully out of sight. Then he tried another pocket and found a tiny folder, cut like a canister, on which was printed in gold the following inscription:

Van Houten's Cocoa, on the tables of the world.
A Perfect Beverage
combining Strength,
Purity, and Solubility.
Open here.

When he opened it, up popped a little paper table set for two: two painted plates, two cups of painted cocoa, two painted sugar buns.

"Very tasty," said the stranger. "Instant breakfast. Want some?"

"No thanks," said Anatole. "I've already eaten mine."

"Put it in your pocket then," said the stranger. "Pockets are a great invention. Did you know my mother was a kangaroo? Perhaps the earth is but a—" He waved his arms histrionically, searching for the word.

"A marble?" suggested Anatole.

"A marble, right! A marble in the pocket of God. When I was a kid, I used to pick pockets in reverse. Instead of taking things out, I put things in. A gumdrop here. A candy cane there. Now how did this ad for Van Houten's cocoa get in my pocket?"

"Maybe you're a traveling salesman," said Anatole.

But the stranger was rummaging through his pockets again. This time he pulled out a silver Maltese cross.

"Now what in the name of heaven is this?" he exclaimed.

"That's a war medal," said Anatole. "Oh, let me look at it. I'm very interested in war. There's writing on the back. E-R-I-K H-A-N-S-O-N."

"Erik Hanson!" shouted the stranger. "Why, I'm Erik Hanson of the 147th Regiment. That's two things I remember."

"Four," said Anatole. "Your mother is a kangaroo and you put things in people's pockets."

"I forgot to tell you—what is your name?"

"Anatole."

"Well, Anatole, I forgot to tell you I'm an awful liar and you can't believe half of what I say. But what army did I serve with, I wonder?"

"Wait right here," said Anatole.

He darted into his house, pulled all the galoshes out of the hall closet, and—wonder of wonders!—there lay his shoebox of lead soldiers, just where he remembered putting it away. Then he ran into the bathroom and grabbed a book that was lying on the radiator. At night in the bathtub he liked to read a chapter from *So You Want to Be a Magician*. And finally he raced back to Erik Hanson, half afraid he would find him gone.

But there he sat, swinging to and fro on Anatole's swing, dragging his feet in the dandelions. Anatole opened

"But there he sat, swinging to and fro on Anatole's swing, dragging his feet in the dandelions."

the box of soldiers to show him, and Erik peered in, very much interested.

"You have a fine collection. I had a wooden soldier when I was a kid. And if you opened him up, you found another one, only smaller. And if you opened *him* up, you found another one, still smaller. The smallest was no bigger than a flea's ear. I never saw it, but I knew it was there. Some things you have to take on faith. Well, Anatole, do you find anyone like me in that box?"

"Here's a soldier in a blue uniform rather like yours," said Anatole, picking one out. "Maybe you're an infantry corporal of the U.S. Army, 1864."

"That would make me awfully old," said Erik, laughing. "Over a hundred."

"How old are you?" asked Anatole.

Erik shrugged. His rough pink skin wrinkled merrily around his eyes. His hair was so pale that you could not tell whether to call it blond or white. He might have been twenty; he might have been fifty.

"I brought out my magic book, too," said Anatole. "It tells how to find things like coins and playing cards. And it's full of nifty magic words. Abracadabra! Puziel, guziel, psdiel, zap!"

"See if there's a chapter on finding lost people," said Erik.

Anatole opened the book.

"Darn it, this isn't my book of magic. It's my book of games."

"Oh, I love games," exclaimed Erik. "What games does your book have?"

"Fox and Goose," read Anatole, flipping through the pages, "Bob-Cherry, Baste the Bear, May I, The Quickest Way of Going to Anywhere . . ."

"What *is* the quickest way?" asked Erik. "I don't know that game."

So Anatole read:

"Let the players write the name of London Town (or the desired destination) on a paper and cast it into the middle of the circle. Then, let them take hands and run around the circle very fast, chanting:

> " 'See saw sacradown,
>   which is the way to London Town?
>   (Insert desired destination.)
>   One foot up and the other foot down,
>   that is the way to London Town.
>   (One journey to a customer.)' "

"That sounds like a magic spell," said Erik. "Ahoy, boys, I'm off to Hawaii!"

"No, it's not a magic spell. It doesn't have any magic words."

"Nonsense," said Erik. "You know why those words don't sound magic? Because we know what they mean. Now if I were a one-eyed bull snake and heard those words, I'd figure they were the most magical things around. Let's write the name of my town on a piece of paper, and then let's draw a circle . . ."

"You don't remember the name of your town," Anatole reminded him.

"Quite true. I forgot. So let's write. 'Erik's home.'"

Anatole ran once more to the house and fetched paper and pencil from the kitchen table and wrote very carefully:

Erik's Home

Under the apple tree, Anatole drew a circle in the grass with his heel and cast down the paper.

"Now, let's take hands," said Erik, "and start running."

And as they ran, they shouted:

> "See saw sacradown
> which is the way to Erik's home?
> One foot up and the other foot down,
> that is the way to Erik's home."

Almost immediately their feet left the ground and sped effortlessly over the tops of the trees and then over the clouds. Anatole found it amazing that his feet, so long accustomed to the ground, could make a road of the air. Through a break in the clouds, Anatole saw the Statue of Liberty. And then he found himself running beside Erik over the open sea.

Waves heaped themselves up and tumbled toward them like mountains, on which the sun shone so brilliantly that you would have thought they were running on silver.

"Look," called Erik, "a boat! Let's give them a scare, shall we?"

An ocean liner was passing them, slowly and steadily, and they ran alongside it so close that Anatole could see men and women dancing in the main ballroom, and he could hear the orchestra playing "Blue Moon." Through a porthole he could look into the kitchen, where two waiters were clinking glasses. The cozy smell of tobacco and cabbage nearly made him cry.

At the back of the ship huddled several passengers in blankets. A child's voice cried out, "I see a man and a boy running on the sea!"

And the grownups all looked up at the broken clouds of the evening sky, for of course that is the reasonable place to find the unexpected shapes of things.

Night came swiftly and swallowed the ship, but a thin crack of light broke on the horizon ahead of them. Then the sun popped up like a luminous peach, silhouetting a fishing boat where three old men rowed toward a distant shore.

"Hey, fishermen," called Erik, "what country is that?"

"Norway," called back the fishermen, who had seen stranger sights in the sea than a man and a boy running on the water. They had not run very long before Anatole spied a ferryboat ahead of them, and as they drew near, they heard childish voices singing:

> "*Ja, vi elsker dette landet*
> Yes, we love this land of ours . . .*"

There on the main deck stood a stout man in uniform, directing a chorus of school children.

"Hey, schoolmaster," called Erik, "what town is that?"

The schoolmaster was too astonished to answer, but

the children cried out joyously, "Fredrikstad, Fredrikstad."

At these words, Anatole felt his feet turn abruptly. Now they carried him over a town of small wooden houses, past a brickyard, and then suddenly his feet stopped, and Anatole tumbled into a new-mown pasture, and Erik tumbled on top of him.

Anatole sat up.

"Erik, where are we?"

Erik's face looked as if the sun had just risen in it.

"In Sellebak. And you won't find it in the *World Atlas,* either. What nerve to call itself a *World Atlas* and not include Sellebak! Do you see that house at the edge of the pasture? I was born in that house. Do you see that tall man standing in the doorway? That's my father. He sailed all over the world when I was little. He's bald as a stone now; he wasn't then. And that small woman beside him, she's my mother. Her hands are tinier than yours, Anatole. I used to play with her gloves in church. Oh, Anatole, I remember, I remember!"

By nightfall, everyone in Sellebak knew that Erik Hanson had returned, bringing with him a boy who was rumored to be a great magician. Friends came all the way from Fredrikstad to see him. To make certain of a warm welcome, each one brought something to eat, until Fru Hanson's kitchen could hold no more baskets of cheese, no more platters of herring and onions and fish cakes, and no more jars of cloudberry jam. Herr Hanson set up a table outside, a safe distance from the gooseberry bushes that were just ripening and a great temptation to the children. Only Anatole noticed the old man who stood by the biggest bush eating gooseberries, as if he thought himself invisible or everyone else blind. He did not seem to belong to any of the visiting families.

Over a bowl of steaming cabbage, Erik remembered part of his story.

"You were eighteen and you enlisted," said his mother, "and I never saw you again. It was a beautiful sunny day in June, just like this one."

"I remember," said Erik. "And I remember growing up in this house. I remember the stove where I loved to warm myself. It had a picture of Vulcan on the door."

"I still have that stove," said his mother, wiping her glasses and blowing her nose.

"And I remember the winter that the hens froze on their perch," said Erik. "And I remember how I loved molasses on brown bread, and you told me how sugar and butter on white bread tasted much better, only there wasn't any."

"That was at the beginning of the war," said Herr Hanson. "Do you remember the peaches I used to send you from America? Tell me, Anatole, do you like peaches?"

"Yes, indeed," said Anatole, taking a second helping of fish cakes.

"Good," said Herr Hanson. "Shows you have good sense. Magic is fine, but I don't understand it. I think perhaps Erik is not quite right in his head; all these stories about running across the ocean. Well, well. We must believe in God and accept what happens."

A stout young woman with a crown of blond braids on her head and a child in her arms came shyly up to Erik.

"Do you remember me, Erik? You promised to marry me once. Well, that was a long time ago, and I married another man. But I still remember the song you sang to me."

And the whole company fell silent as she sang, slowly and clearly:

"How lovely is your golden hair,
blessed is he who can win you."

The sun danced in the leaves of the plum tree, and Fru Hanson wiped her glasses.

"That was thirty years ago," said Erik. "I remember all of you. I remember the day I went off to fight. But of that thirty years between that day and this, I remember nothing."

He stood up and walked around the yard, whispering, "Thirty years lost! Thirty years lost! What I wouldn't give to see them again!"

And Anatole, stumbling after him, bumped smack into the old man who was still helping himself to the ripe gooseberries.

"Excuse me," said Anatole.

"So you wish to turn back the sun," called the old man to Erik. "Then it's to the sun you must go, my lad. My great-grandfather journeyed there once."

"Is it possible?" exclaimed Erik.

"Not for you," said the old man, laughing. "The sun speaks only to children. If anyone can find the sun's house, it's this boy here. But the way is long and very difficult."

"Very difficult?" asked Anatole, who loved a good adventure if it was not too dangerous.

"Of course," said the old man, "but there are always people who want to make the journey because there are always people who want to be magicians."

"Can the sun make me into a magician?"

The old man shook his head. "The sun won't, but the journey will. It's the journeys we make for others that give us the power to change ourselves. The hardest part is getting home again, for you can't go home the way you left it. Nobody can give you the magic to take you home. You have to find that magic on your own."

"Oh, Anatole," exclaimed Erik, "say you'll go."

"Of course you can always be an ordinary magician who pulls rabbits out of hats and doves out of handkerchiefs," said the old man.

"No," said Anatole, "I want to be a real magician. How do I find the house of the sun?"

The old man looked very pleased. "I will give you some runes to say."

"Runes?" asked Anatole, puzzled. "What are runes?"

The old man smiled. "Runes are the magic words of the old gods who lived here before the Christians came."

"I love magic words," said Anatole.

"Yes, I could tell that at a glance. And so these words will probably disappoint you. They are perfectly clear, and yet they make no sense. They are important, yet they teach you nothing. Do you see that hill just beyond the pasture, across the road?"

"I see it. Erik and I landed near there."

"If you stand on that hill and say the runes aloud, one of the four winds will come to help you. I don't know which one. A fair wind is a great help in reaching the house of the sun. If you are in trouble, say the runes backward. But you can only use the runes in this way once."

"Thirty years! I shall have my thirty years again!" crowed Erik.

"Tell me the runes," begged Anatole.

The old man put his mouth close to Anatole's ear so that Erik shouldn't hear him.

"9 were Nothe's sisters:
Then the 9 was 8
and the 8 was 7
and the 7 was 6
and the 6 was 5
and the 5 was 4
and the 4 was 3
and the 3 was 2
and the 2 was 1
and the 1 was none."

"Who are Nothe's sisters?" asked Anatole.

"They are the nine stars who bring in the night. They're bringing it in now, though we can't see it coming yet. Better hurry, for if the night catches you, you'll never find your way home."

"Good-bye, Erik," said Anatole, beginning to feel a little anxious.

And to his amazement, Erik lifted him off the ground and kissed him.

"If I can help you, Anatole, call me. If you need a war fought or a field plowed—"

"I'll come straight to you," Anatole promised.

And he set off with great strides across the pasture for fear the smell of Fru Hanson's savory pancakes would make him turn back.

The hill looked at him the way any hill at home would look at him; it said, *Climb me.* Anatole started to climb, stepping carefully in his sneakers over the slabs of stone that broke like wrinkled faces through the grass. When he reached the top, he saw he was standing where four pastures met. To the east and the south, he saw clusters of white houses dreaming on the horizon, with an uncertain road glinting between them. To the west sparkled a church as white and small as a tooth. To the north rose another hill.

Anatole stood on a rock and said gravely:

"9 were Nothe's sisters:
Then the 9 was 8
and the 8 was 7
and the 7 was 6
and the 6 was 5
and the 5 was 4
and the 4 was 3
and the 3 was 2
and the 2 was 1
and the 1 was none."

Nothing happened.

A flock of gulls fluttered down like handkerchiefs into the pasture. Then all at once Anatole spied a tiny speck in the sky that, as it flew nearer, took the shape first of a bird and then of an angel. But what, thought Anatole, could it be?

It was a man in a suit as white as snow and as bright as water, and he was riding a book, and when he saw Anatole, he sang out, "Who called the west wind?"

"Me," said Anatole, abashed at this strange figure. "I want to go to the house of the sun."

"And what will you do when you find it?" asked the west wind.

"I'll ask the sun to give Erik Hanson his thirty lost years and to send me home again, for I can't go home the way I came."

The west wind opened his book, which was the sad color of twilight, and turned the pages one by one. They gave off a most pleasant perfume, which Anatole saw came not from the paper but from the letters printed there. A castle and vineyard glowed in a sunlit D; the harvesters were carrying baskets of grapes on their heads, and Anatole could hear the women singing, though he could not understand the words. A formal garden grew in a shady O; the gardener tying back the delphiniums glanced up at Anatole and tipped his hat.

When the west wind had turned every page, he closed the book, and the music stopped abruptly and the fragrance of the flowers disappeared.

"The house of the sun," he said thoughtfully. "To tell

"It was a man in a suit as white as snow and as bright as water, and he was riding a book . . ."

you the truth, I don't know the way, but I'll take you to
my brother the north wind, who is stronger than I and
flies farther."

Together they flew north, over pine forests and over
the camps of the Lapps following the reindeer and over the
ice fields to the top of the world, and alit on the roof of the
biggest palace Anatole had ever seen. A hundred turrets,
he figured, and two hundred flags stiff as postcards; five
hundred diamond windows at least, chimneys thick as a
forest, and everything cut from blue ice.

"The door is always frozen shut," said the west wind.
"We must fly down the great chimney."

"What is the great chimney?" asked Anatole.

"Wait and see."

Down the chimney they flew and crawled out of an
ice fireplace into an enormous room. It had no furniture
at all, nothing but a giant tree growing out of the floor to
the ceiling. Perched on the lowest branch slept an eagle.

"Brother, wake up," urged the west wind. "This boy
wants to find the house of the sun. Farewell!"

And the west wind flew back up the chimney.

The north wind opened his eyes. "You will find the
house of the sun at the top of this tree."

"How far is it to the top?" asked Anatole, who loved
to climb trees.

"I do not know. But halfway up takes a hundred years.
Are you a hero of the golden age?"

"I don't think so," said Anatole.

"Well, it's worth finding out. Climb till you come to a
golden city nestled in the branches of the tree. It belongs to

the sun's own finches, which sing to him day and night.
Knock at the gate and ask for the magic drum that will
carry you to the house of the sun. And if they give you the
drum, sit on it and say, 'Drum, drum, fly to the sun,' and
it will take you there directly. Only do not be afraid of
anything you meet on the way."

"Thank you," said Anatole.

The trunk of the tree grew thick as a wall. Anatole
could not even see where it curved around to the other side.
He looked up into the branches. No light broke through
at the top. The tree grew into a great darkness.

"It's best not to think about the top," said the north
wind. "It's best just to start climbing."

So Anatole put his foot on the first low branch and
sprang up into the tree.

At first he found the climbing fun. He met nobody
on the way except two squirrels who chattered to him,
"What news?" Anatole smiled and shook his head. And
then, as he had no one else to talk to, he talked to himself.

"It's just like climbing the big pine tree in Grandma
and Grandpa's yard. When I was real little, it seemed like
I'd never get to the top. Now I can shimmy up there easy,
and I can look down and see Mr. Pederson across the street,
mowing the lawn."

Though he squinted, he could see nothing beyond the
branches that surrounded him. They seemed to stretch out
forever, and the discovery made him feel lonely and a little
scared.

"Oh, but I'm not alone. Lots of things live in trees.
All kinds of birds make nests in trees—"

He broke off. He did not like to think of all the things that might live in this one. He wanted, very badly, a peanut-butter and jelly sandwich and a nice saggy sofa to lie down on, like the one at home. He sank so deeply into this thought that he nearly forgot to hold onto the branch. That frightened him; he stopped, trembling, and sat down to rest. And in the silence of his resting he heard a thin cold sound.

"Hsssss! Hsssss!"

Quickly he glanced up. No wind blew, but the leaves shook. Behind them white blossoms nodded to him. Blossoms or—he drew his hand back in alarm. What he had taken for blossoms was a tangle of snakes, smiling and darting their tongues at him. And now that he was afraid, they drew closer to him, whispering, *"Hssssss. Hssssss. Just you wait. Just you wait."*

He jumped up and climbed away from them, but the branches sprang back as fast as he pushed them aside. When he could not move forward or backward, he sat down again, wondering what to do. The branches locked him into the darkness. He listened for the snakes. He did not hear them, but something else waited behind the leaves and saw his fear and growled softly.

The wind rocked the branch he was sitting on, and he held it tightly, for he saw just behind the leaves, and very close to him, the faces of hideous dogs. Their eyes glowed like candles, and it seemed to Anatole that the whole tree was burning. Far off he heard the yelping of foxes and the cries of hunters.

With all his might, Anatole pushed himself through

the thicket, closing his eyes so that he wouldn't have to look at the dogs. And who knows where he might have ended up if he hadn't bumped against a golden gate, set in a smooth golden wall that shone like a crown.

A goldfinch wearing a silver ruff opened the gate.

"Excuse me," said Anatole hastily, for the goldfinch immediately tried to shut it again, "have you the drum that flies to the sun?"

"Are you the one that's to have it?" asked the goldfinch.

"Yes," said Anatole.

"Who sent you?"

"The north wind."

"Very well, I'll fetch it," said the goldfinch. "You may wait in my sentry box if you like. I've a bottle of dandelion wine on my desk. Help yourself. Have one for the road."

Before he could do so, the goldfinch returned bearing the drum in its claws.

"Don't jump off the drum till you reach the house of the sun. The moment you leave it, it will return to us."

"I'll be most careful," said Anatole.

He climbed on the drum and said, "Drum, drum, fly to the sun."

Immediately the drum swooped up and out of the tree, broke through the sky, and landed on a long white road in a broad, bare country. The road toward which the drum carried him ended at the door of a most peculiar house. It shone clear as glass and looked exactly like a pumpkin that has grown from a sunbeam. As the drum bumped along the road, an old woman appeared in the doorway.

"Well, well," said the old woman, "what have we here?"

Anatole jumped off the drum and whoosh! it vanished.

"I'm looking for the sun," said Anatole.

"Well, well," said the old woman, "I happen to be his mother. What do you want with him?"

"I want him to give Erik Hanson his thirty lost years and to send me home again, for I don't know the way and I can't go home the way I came."

"And what will you give me if I take you to see him?"

Anatole plunged his hands into his pockets. Nothing, nothing. No, wait, what was this? He pulled out the little advertisement for Van Houten's cocoa.

"A little book, is it?" inquired the old woman. "What's it called?"

"Van Houten's Cocoa," Anatole read bravely. "A Perfect Beverage combining Strength, Purity, and Solubility. Open here." He wanted to weep.

"It's magic, of course," said the old woman. "Otherwise you wouldn't have brought it. You would have brought me a cartload of pearls drawn by unicorns or a bushel of singing rubies. Such toys I see every day. But rarely does anyone bring me a magic book called *Van Houten's Cocoa*. What does it do?"

Anatole shook his head.

"Come, come. Does it turn rain into tigers? Princes into cabbages?"

"No," said Anatole.

And then he remembered the runes. So he put the little folder to his lips and over it he whispered:

"and the none was 1
and the 1 was 2
and the 2 was 3
and the 3 was 4
and the 4 was 5
and the 5 was 6
and the 6 was 7
and the 7 was 8
and the 8 was 9;
9 were Nothe's sisters."

"It's all or nothing," he added, and he opened the folder.

But instead of a tiny paper table set for two, there sprang forth a huge table set for forty. And such a setting! Wands of cowslip bread, platters of candied violets and marzipan marigolds, great tureens of daffodil soup and crocks of rose-petal jam. And in the middle, of course, stood a silver urn of cocoa from which flew a little pennant: *Van Houten's. On the table of the sun.*

"Oh, that's killing," cried the old woman, "perfectly killing! It's the best toy anyone has ever given me. Let me try it."

She shut the folder and the banquet disappeared.

She opened it and the banquet returned. The bread was still warm. Anatole had never smelled anything so delicious.

"Well, well," said the old woman, seizing a loaf and biting into it, "help yourself."

"Thank you," said Anatole. He ate two loaves of bread and three plates of violets, and then he laughed. What if his mother, who was always saying, "Eat, eat," could see him now! He felt so much better that he began to believe things would go well for him after all.

"What about the sun?" he inquired.

"Ah," said the old woman, "he's shining over Asia. Would you like to watch him?"

She led Anatole into the round glass house. In the middle gleamed a pool of water, and in that still water he saw the sun, but how different the sun looked in this mirror than in the skies at home. No moving ball of fire but an old man the color of embers, wearing a raven on each shoulder, and with each step he took, he grew older still.

"He'll be half dead when he arrives," said the old woman, "and that is the time to catch him, for that's when he's the wisest. You must meet him on the road, for when he passes through the doorway of this house, he will turn into a little child, and then there's no seriousness in him at all, and he won't help you a bit."

So Anatole, sipping his cocoa, watched for the old man on the road. But the old woman saw farther than Anatole.

"That's he," she said. "Run to him quickly before he reaches the door."

Anatole bounded out of the house and down the road till he met the sun, who was creeping along, white-haired, squint-eyed, and more wrinkled than the sea. "Grack! Grack!" clucked the ravens on his shoulders.

"Sun!" called Anatole.

The sun peered all around him.

"Where are you?" he croaked. "I don't see well now, and my hearing is bad."

"I've come to ask you about Erik Hanson."

"Erik Hanson of Sellebak?" said the sun. "What about him?"

"He's lost thirty years of his life, and he wants them back."

"Well, he can't have them," said the sun crossly. "I won't give him time, but I will give him knowledge. He shall know everything that happened to him during those years. Will that do?"

"I guess it will have to do," said Anatole.

"I will send him my servants, Thought and Memory, my two trusty ravens who tell me all that goes on in the great world. They will show him his past. They'll show him how to turn hurts into blessings and dragons into princesses. And if he listens to them, he will be the greatest storyteller in Norway."

"He's a good storyteller right now," said Anatole, remembering how Erik once described his mother as a kangaroo.

"But if he does not want this knowledge," continued the sun, "he should send my servants away. Sometimes people forget what it causes them pain to remember. It is not easy for a soldier to remember the faces of the people he has killed."

They had arrived at the door, and no sooner had the sun passed through it than zzzzzz! the old man vanished and there stood a child, scarcely a year old, babbling and laughing and tumbling on the floor.

The old woman dipped the corner of her apron in

the pool and scrubbed the child's face, and snatching a loaf of bread from the table, she pushed it into his hand.

"And now, outside with you. You must go and wake the children in Brazil."

"Wait!" cried Anatole. "You must tell me how to get home again."

But the sun ran laughing out the door.

"That's a pity," said the old woman, shaking her head. "Now you'll have to wander the earth until you find your road, for the sun talks to a man only once in his life, and you've had your chance."

Anatole burst into tears. But suddenly he felt a flutter of wings brush his cheek, and there on his shoulder sat the sun's raven.

"I am Thought," cawed the raven, "and I offer you my services. You cannot return home the way you came, by drum, by tree, or by wind, for the connections are uncertain and none of them runs on time. But I am swifter than the drum and the wind, and I am not rooted in any one place like the tree."

"What must I do?" asked Anatole.

"Think of your home. A real magician isn't afraid of what he doesn't understand. You are a real magician now."

So Anatole thought of his house and his swing and his mother singing "Awake, Ye Wintry Earth," and how she would soon go to the kitchen and start supper, meat loaf, maybe, and he thought how his papa would come home with a newspaper for himself and a gingerbread man for Anatole from the bakery, and he thought how no place was nicer than this place where two people loved him.

*"The old woman dipped the corner of her apron in the pool
and scrubbed the child's face . . ."*

And he found himself sitting on his swing at twilight.

But this is not the end of the story. Two days before Christmas, early in the morning, Anatole saw a large black bird drop something on the windowsill outside his room. He opened the window and found a reindeer's tooth, which he recognized, and a book, which he did not. On the cover he read *Erik Hanson's Saga*. And inscribed on the flyleaf was the following message:

How can I ever thank you, dear Anatole? Here are the stories that Memory has told me and Thought has helped me to set down. The book is full of magic words, and they'll bring you many adventures if you take the trouble to learn what they mean.

Love, Erik

SAILING
TO CYTHERA

Grandmother never threw anything away. If you left a seashell under the piano at Christmas, you knew it would still be there when you went to visit in June. Whenever Anatole complained that he couldn't find his sneakers or his dump truck, Grandma said, "You wouldn't believe the stuff I've lost in this house. But everything turns up in the wash. You go and play."

So he did. First he sewed on her sewing machine.

Then he wound her five clocks: a grandfather clock, a cuckoo clock, a clock set in the bosom of a brass stork, an alarm clock, and a porcelain clock with a ring of parrots dancing on its face under a glass dome. No two clocks kept exactly the same time, which was fine, said Grandma, because no two people do either.

Then he asked her if he could play kingdom and use her gold filigree candy dish for a crown.

"That's been lost for months," said Grandma.

Then he asked if he could play with her two silver birds that held salt and pepper.

"When they turn up," said Grandma.

Then he drummed on the piano, for it is very difficult to lose a piano. He played "The Frog He Would A-Wooing Go" with his big toe for Pizzicato, Grandma's black cat, who did not like children and who slept all day in front of the fireplace. Grandma always kept a fire burning, even in summer.

"Nothing is cozier than a fire," said Grandma, who did not have to chop wood for her fires but only to light the little jet over the grate and turn the gold key on the hearth and behold! out leaped two magnificent flames. Anatole called it magic. Grandma called it "natural gas."

"There are only two things you mustn't do," said Grandma. "Don't try to light the fireplace by yourself. Your mother singed her eyebrows off doing that when she was your age. And don't write on the wallpaper. It's very old. It came with the house."

"Can I touch the wallpaper?" asked Anatole.

Grandmother laughed.

"Of course you can! I touch it all the time. I can't really enjoy a thing unless I can touch it, can you?"

The wallpaper, which covered all the rooms in the house, showed a river dotted with islands where shepherds and shepherdesses danced and rowed about in small boats garlanded with roses. The shepherds, in blue coats and russet breeches, leaned pensively on golden crooks. The shepherdesses nodded like peonies ruffled by the wind and smiled under their broad straw hats. Some wore masks and some wore fantastic wigs hung with small trumpets and shells.

And far beyond them, so faint you could scarcely make it out, glittered a bridge and the towers of a city.

And when you had seen all this, you saw it again, for the pattern repeated itself over and over again, except for the bridge and the city, which only occurred over the umbrella stand in the front hall.

"Who are those people?" asked Anatole, sitting beside his grandmother on the stairs.

"This woman I call Madame d'Aulnoy," said Grandma, pointing to a buxom woman in enormous pink skirts and a satin stomacher. "You can see she's sensible; she's not wearing a wig. And this girl in the rowboat is her daughter, Thérèse. And here's where I spilled the chicken soup I was carrying up to Grandpa when he was sick. It's the very shape of a dragon."

And suddenly she started to sing:

> "On the bridge of Avignon
> they are dancing, they are dancing,
> On the bridge of Avignon
> they are dancing, every one."

"I like that song," said Anatole.

"That's all I remember learning in fourth grade," said Grandma. "That and Frère Jacques. I must have learned more, but the rest escapes me."

Every warm evening after supper, Grandma helped Grandpa into the big wicker chair on the back porch and surrounded him with pillows. Anatole brought him the newspaper, and then he and Grandma sat together on the swing, cool in the shadow of the honeysuckle bush that pressed against the screen. Nobody said much. Anatole chewed a cinnamon-stick cigar. Then Grandma, incited by the smell of cinnamon, fetched ginger ale for Grandpa and Anatole and fixed a cup of Sanka for herself because she'd lost the canister of tea. And when she picked up the empty glasses, she tested the left arm of Grandpa's chair, which wobbled.

"Jon will fix it. He can fix anything. A man like that is one in a million."

"Where does Jon go every evening?" asked Anatole one day.

"Down to the Schiller Inn for a mug of beer."

"Don't we have any beer?" asked Anatole.

"No," said Grandma. "I don't like it at all, except for the foam on top. That's the part I like. Don't let me forget about that armrest."

And they would all forget until the next evening.

Jon lived in the spare room and helped take care of Grandpa, who was twenty years older than Grandma and had forgotten how to walk. Sometimes he could not remember Anatole's name, but he always remembered to smile at him. Sometimes he said peculiar things like "Isn't it time to light the lamps?" or "Isn't it time to meet the boat?"

Then Grandma would kiss him and say, "Did you ever hear such nonsense? Grandpa, who do you love?"

"You," said Grandpa, taking Grandma's hand.

And then they heard the front door slam, and Grandma would say, "Jon's home. It's eight o'clock. Time for you to go to bed."

What Anatole minded about going to bed was the dark space under the bed. The bed stood in the room where his mother had slept as a child, and his mother's dolls still sat on the high shelves over the chest of drawers. Their china heads gleamed and their glass eyes followed him about. The ceiling had stars pasted on it, and the stars glowed in the dark. He would have preferred another room, but Grandma always put him in this one, and he didn't want to admit he was afraid.

He had found a way of climbing into bed that helped a little. If he sprang from the door straight across the floor, he reached the bed in a single bound, so that the dark space under the bed hardly even saw him coming.

Then he waited until Grandma came in and sang to him, for when the sun lazed in the trees outside, Anatole had trouble falling asleep, and on the longest day of the year, which Grandmother called "Midsummer's Eve," he couldn't sleep at all, although she'd let him stay up an hour later than usual.

On that night he lay wrapped in his bathrobe, wide awake, waiting. Nobody came. He heard Jon's footsteps in the hall, and he called out, "Where's Grandma?"

Jon stuck his head through the door. "You still awake?"

Anatole nodded.

"You want a glass of water?"

"I want Grandma to come and sing to me."

"She can't," said Jon. "Have a toothpick."

"Why not?" asked Anatole, sticking the toothpick into his mouth.

"She's watching Lawrence Welk. The band is playing

'Let Me Call You Sweetheart,' and that's her favorite. Tell you what. I'll sing to you." He sat down on the bed. "What does she sing?"

" 'On the Bridge of Avignon.' "

"Don't know that one," said Jon.

" 'Nearer My God to Thee.' "

"Tell you what," said Jon, sitting down in the rocker. "Let me sing you one I picked up while I was herding sheep in Nevada."

"Is it about sheep?"

And Jon sang, in a scratchy voice that sounded as if he'd kept it closed up in a pickle bottle for years:

> "What'll we do with a drunken sailor,
> What'll we do with a drunken sailor,
> What'll we do with a drunken sailor,
> Early in the morning?
>
> "Pull out the plug and wet him all over,
> Pull out the plug and wet him all over,
> Pull out the plug and wet him all over,
> Early in the morning."

And when Anatole looked at the wallpaper over his bed, he thought he saw, far away, a one-masted schooner and the drunken sailor, quite drenched, sleeping on a pile of rigging.

Outside the window, the sun dropped slowly behind roofs and chimneys and the feathery tops of trees. But a bright stillness quickened everything in the room, and Jon, who hated to end the song, turned it into a new one.

> "The water is wide,
> I cannot cross it,
> and neither have I wings to fly—"

He yawned hugely and sang the last stanzas with his eyes shut.

> "Give me a boat that can carry two,
> and both shall row, my true love and I."

And Anatole could see the True Love in her little rowboat, fluttering her handkerchief at him, and now her boat bumped against Jon's shoulder, but he sat as quiet as a mountain, for he had fallen asleep, silhouetted against a light that was breaking over the water, brighter and brighter. The sun was rising in the country of the wallpaper.

The True Love, in a green tunic with flowers in her hair, motioned Anatole toward the boat.

"Hurry, or we'll miss the fair, and the boat to Cythera will leave without us!"

Anatole got in and sat down. He was too bewildered to ask, "What fair?" and "Where is Cythera?" How queer it felt to drift behind the chest of drawers! He saw that Grandma's French dictionary had fallen behind it and lay covered with dust. The dolls looked longingly after him, like friends waving him off on a long journey.

"Your costume is lovely," said the True Love. "Did you get it at Auberge's?"

"The dolls looked longingly after him, like friends waving him off on a long journey."

Anatole looked down at his bathrobe.

"My grandmother gave it to me."

"And who's your grandmother?" asked the True Love.

And though he knew she had another name besides "grandmother," he could not remember it for the life of him. "She lives back there, over the water," he answered, trying to sound casual. "Are you Madame d'Aulnoy?"

The True Love burst out laughing.

"I beg your pardon, Madame d'Aulnoy is my mother. If you will not tell me your grandmother's name, perhaps you will tell me yours."

But to his alarm, Anatole found that he could not remember his own name, either! The comfortable furniture of his room was rapidly vanishing, like a skyline of untenanted buildings. The True Love dipped her oars in and out, and water lilies sank away under the boat and popped up on the other side. The air smelled deliciously of flowers and cinnamon. Suddenly he remembered a name. It was not his own, but he said it anyway.

"Frère Jacques."

The True Love clapped her hands.

"Oh, you're a monk, of course. I should have guessed. Now you must ask me who I am."

"Are you Thérèse?"

"No, no, you must look at my costume. Can't you tell who I am?"

Anatole stared at her sandals and the bow and quiverful of arrows resting on her shoulder. She was very pretty, and she was chewing a blond spit curl that had escaped her crown of violets.

"No, I can't guess," he said at last.

"It is not polite to say *no*. You must say, 'I beg your pardon.'"

"I beg your pardon," said Anatole.

"I forgive you. I am Diana of the Hunt today, so I must forgive everyone who asks me. Do you think I am beautiful?"

"Yes," said Anatole, suddenly embarrassed.

"Thank you. You may call me Thérèse if you like."

The boat was gliding over the pebbly nests of half a dozen fish. Frogs sat like pulsing emeralds under the elderberry bushes on the banks. Suddenly a flock of orioles flashed overhead, and Anatole heard a burst of trumpets.

"Look," cried Thérèse, "on the bridge, everyone is dancing! Here, take an oar."

Pulling his oar hard as they rounded the bend, he saw over his shoulder hundreds of boats moored along the shore and just beyond them the bridge with its broad arches standing in the water and its delicate crown of booths and flags sparkling on top. And on the other side of the bridge he saw a ship, carved like a huge scallop, garlanded with roses. A thin sail fluttered from the single mast.

"Whose boat is that?" asked Anatole.

"That boat belongs to the Emperor of the Moon. That's the boat to Cythera."

"And where is Cythera?" asked Anatole.

But Thérèse seemed not to hear.

The boat nosed gently into the reeds. Thérèse jumped out, and Anatole tied it to a large honeysuckle bush. Shepherds and shepherdesses were hurrying up the grassy hill to the fair.

"And now you must take my arm," said Thérèse.

As they crested the hill, the fair blossomed before them. Stalls and shops packed the narrow street. The air glittered with handkerchiefs and silks, sausages and sea-shells, feathers and flowers, butterflies and candlesticks and tambourines. An old woman dozed behind a mountain of melons.

"Life, life!" shouted the wine merchant, pushing through the crowd with a casket of brandy on his back.

"Knives sharpened!"

"Mend your bellows, mister?"

"Teeth pulled here!"

"Here's health," cried the watercress woman, "two francs a bunch!"

Anatole ducked to avoid a girl carrying a tray of milk pots on her head.

"Ah, there's a puppet show," said Thérèse. "Let's go watch. And look as if you think I am very beautiful."

"But I do think so," protested Anatole.

Thérèse stamped her foot.

"What good is that to me if the others don't see it?"

They jostled themselves a place close to the front. A man dressed in rags and bells was packing away the puppets, but the curtain rose on a tableau of trained dogs, who sat at a table and ate with knives and forks. Anatole clapped hard. Thérèse was not watching. She kept glancing at a clown in a white suit who shambled over to them, his mandolin under his arm.

"Hello, Gilles," Thérèse greeted him, curling her lip as if she didn't like him a bit. "This is my friend, Frère Jacques."

Anatole smiled and felt someone lay an arm around his shoulder and draw him aside. He turned and met the eyes of a red-faced fellow dressed all in stripes like peppermint candy, who whispered into his ear, "May I introduce myself? Mezzetin is the name, sir, friend of Gilles and the lady Thérèse. And now may I warn you to leave Mademoiselle Thérèse as soon as possible?"

"But why?" asked Anatole.

"Because she is determined to take the ship to Cythera, sir, a trip as dangerous as it is foolish. The Blimlim raised a storm last night, and three ships sank in the waters off Cythera."

"What," said Anatole, "is the Blimlim?"

Mezzetin lowered his voice still more, so that Anatole could scarcely hear him.

"The Blimlim is a monster who lives on the island. No one has seen him, sir, but you may read about him in the old histories. He has the body of a lizard, the head of an eagle, the wings of an albatross, and he's as big as a house—"

"Wait," interrupted Anatole. "If no one has seen him, how do you know he's there?"

"Surely you know that you don't have to see someone to know he's there," whispered Mezzetin.

Anatole thought of the dark space under his bed.

"Then why does anyone go to Cythera?" he asked, drawing back a little, for Mezzetin smelled strongly of garlic.

"Because the emperor has offered half his kingdom to the person who will bring him the skin of the Blimlim. And the island itself is a paradise, sir. No one grows old there. A race of children, winged like birds, lives in the air over the island, and they fill it with the most marvelous singing. The pebbles are pearls. The mermaids—"

He was drowned out by applause for a woman dancing with a sword in her mouth. A one-legged soldier sidled up to Anatole and held out a scimitar.

"Alms, kind sir. Do you want to buy this sword? I slew a dozen Turks with it."

"I don't think much of that," said Gilles. "It's easy to hurt somebody. It's very hard to love them." And he rolled his eyes sadly at Thérèse.

"Isn't it time to meet the boat?" said Thérèse. "Come, Frère Jacques. I know *you* aren't afraid."

"I should prefer to grow old than to be eaten by a Blimlim," snapped Mezzetin. "Good-bye."

"I'm going with Thérèse," said Gilles.

The three of them hurried into the crowd that was gathering on the shore. A man in a suit of pearls crossed the little gangplank and led the way into the ship.

"He's the Emperor of the Moon," said Thérèse with a sigh. "Isn't he splendid?"

Thousands of white handkerchiefs fluttered from the top of the bridge. As the ship sailed slowly down the river, a shepherd stopped strumming his mandolin under the willow trees and threw his cap in the air. His sheep, nibbling at the roses that festooned a ruined pavilion, lifted their heads in surprise. Then the cheering faded, the mist of distance blurred the bridge, and the ship entered the open sea.

The passengers paraded up and down the deck, laughing and chattering. At the back of the ship, the drunken sailor lay snoring on the coil of ropes. Anatole knew him at once and sat down beside him. A party of dancers dressed as apes strolled by them. Perhaps they really are apes, thought Anatole. But no, that white cat curled at the feet of the drunken sailor would not be washing itself so lazily.

"Hello, cat," said Anatole. "I have a cat like you at home." The cat stopped washing, its paw poised in the air.

"I am sure your cat is not at all like me, for I belong to Madame d'Aulnoy, and I speak nine languages."

"Is Madame d'Aulnoy on board?"

"She's right over there," answered the cat, "watching us."

And seeing that they had noticed her, a large woman with sharp features and kind eyes stepped away from the railing and held out her hands to Anatole.

"You are a stranger," she said. "Have you come to conquer the Blimlim?"

"No—I mean, I beg your pardon," stammered Anatole.

Madame d'Aulnoy stooped down and held his face in her hands. Rings blazed on her fingers, and her dress, woven all of peacock feathers, dazzled his eyes.

"I'm not laughing at you," she said gravely. "I believe no one but a child can conquer the Blimlim. The emperor's soldiers won't try, not even for half the kingdom. 'We can't fight a mystery,' the captain said to me the other day. 'We have to know what weapons to use, guns or swords or traps.' I will tell you a secret," she whispered into his ear. "The real prize of the island is the golden bough. I would give anything just to see it, and the garden where it grows."

"Land ahoy!" shouted the drunken sailor in his sleep.

The cat jumped up on Anatole's shoulder. Everyone rushed to the front of the boat, and Anatole caught sight of Gilles and Thérèse.

"Frère Jacques," she called, "where have you been? Let's watch for mermaids. Mamma says the weather is just right."

Ahead of them shimmered the island, as green as the first leaves of spring misting over bare trees. Half a dozen horses trotting along the beach ran off into the woods. The boat seemed to be entering a golden twilight that was not of the world it had come from.

"How close night is to morning," said Gilles with a sigh.

"Does it ever get dark here?" Anatole asked the cat.

"Of course. We could put up lanterns as we do on the mainland. But because of the Blimlim we generally leave."

"I'd like to ride those horses we saw."

"They're wild," said the cat. "They live in the garden of the golden bough. I should advise you to leave them alone. Good-bye." And it sprang into the arms of Madame d'Aulnoy.

The boat hushed against the sand. One by one, as if entering a dance, the passengers climbed ashore. Anatole felt Madame d'Aulnoy touch his shoulder.

"Come, little Frère Jacques. You can join our party by the fountain of Venus."

"Please," said Anatole, "I want to go exploring."

Madame d'Aulnoy nodded.

"The other side of the island is wild, and if I were

your mother, I should advise you not to go there. As I am not your mother, let me tell you only that it is very dangerous and very beautiful, and we sail for the mainland at sunset."

The moment she turned to leave, Anatole sprinted past the fountain into the forest beyond it. How glorious everything smelled! Violets and columbine sprang over the rocks, water trickled under the roots at his feet, and farther off the laughter of his friends by the fountain seemed to follow him.

"I'd like to find that garden," said Anatole to himself.

The words were hardly out of his mouth when a white horse stepped into his path and knelt down in front of him. Anatole jumped on its back at once, for he remembered that the horses lived in the garden. Now the quest seemed so simple to him that he wondered why nobody else had tried it. High in the trees overhead he heard a thin singing that sounded more seashell than human.

"That must be the flying children Mezzetin spoke of," he decided, but though he looked carefully and listened hard, he could neither see them nor make out the words of their song.

Directly ahead of him the trees grew much bigger and stood so close together that the horse could pass through them only with difficulty, as if it were entering a fortress. The air turned colder, and a deep silence dropped over everything.

"Horse," he said softly, "are you very close to—"

But he never finished, for something tremendous crashed through the trees behind them. The horse reared up, and Anatole tumbled into a bramble thicket.

"Horse, wait for me!" he called.

The horse was gone. Anatole could not even hear its hoofbeats. He scrambled to his feet and there, waiting to be noticed, crouched the Blimlim. Its green body glittered like a splendid coat of mail, its eyes flickered like bonfires, and its wings eclipsed the land of the light. It had claws like a lion and whiskers like a catfish, and it wore a gold filigree crown on its head.

"Don't run off," hissed the Blimlim. "Stay, and I'll give you a present. I'm sure I have something in my cave you'd like."

Anatole was so thankful not to be eaten up that he did not run. The Blimlim flashed away into the darkness, and soon there came the clatter of somebody opening and shutting many doors.

"Are you still there?" called the Blimlim.

"Yes," Anatole called back.

Instantly the Blimlim reappeared, carrying a cup and saucer on its head.

"Perhaps you'd like some tea," it suggested. It lifted one wing, and out dropped a canister of Earl Grey tea. "Or don't you like tea? What do you like?"

"Ginger ale," said Anatole.

"To tell you the truth, I don't like tea, either. Wait. Don't go away."

It flickered out of sight and returned bearing a pair of sneakers in one claw and a dump truck in the other.

"These look about your size," it said cheerfully.

"Why, there's my truck," exclaimed Anatole, "and

"He scrambled to his feet and there, waiting to be noticed, crouched the Blimlim."

those are my sneakers! Where on earth did you find them?"

"The tide washed them in," answered the Blimlim. "Every morning I comb the beach for treasures. Sometimes I throw things back." The Blimlim flung the tea canister high into the sky. "When I throw them with all my might, they don't return."

They both watched the canister disappear over the horizon.

"A penny for your thoughts," hissed the Blimlim.

"I was thinking that the emperor has offered half his kingdom for your skin," said Anatole.

The Blimlim snorted.

"My skin won't fit him," it said scornfully. And then its green skin turned pale as water.

"Did you come here to capture me?"

"No," said Anatole. "I came to see the garden and the golden bough."

"Oh, it's a lovely garden," exclaimed the Blimlim, much relieved. "Let me take you there. Climb on my head."

Clutching his sneakers and his dump truck, Anatole climbed into the space between its ears, where he could not help noticing how much its gold filigree crown resembled his grandmother's lost candy dish. The Blimlim glided into a hedge that clicked shut behind them, like teeth locking together.

"Now," whispered the Blimlim proudly as he lowered his head for Anatole to dismount, "look!"

Above the water, which gushed from a crystal grotto, the golden bough rose straight up like a tree of heaven. It gave off a light so brilliant that Anatole had to shade his eyes. The leaves did not shake and sigh in the wind, for there was no wind. All around the tree glowed beds of daffodils and roses, lilies and marigolds, and fruit trees of every kind.

"The golden bough grows only in this garden," said the Blimlim. "If you moved it, the bough would die. Tell me, have you ever seen marigolds to equal these? Each flower is a perfect topaz."

Anatole touched one, then drew his hand away, for the flowers felt cold and hard.

"They're all right, but you should smell the marigolds in my grandmother's garden."

"And these apples," continued the Blimlim. "Giant rubies. They never lose their beauty. Do you like rubies?"

"Rubies are O.K.," agreed Anatole, "but you should taste the apples in my grandmother's garden. So juicy and sweet, I wish I had one right now. But your garden is very nice, too," he added hastily, for he was afraid of hurting the Blimlim's feelings.

"Yes, indeed, it's a lovely garden," said the Blimlim.

"But lonely, maybe," said Anatole.

The Blimlim sighed. "Very lonely. I'd move to the mainland at once if I could find a nice dark space where nobody would disturb me."

"I know of a nice dark space," said Anatole.

"Where?"

"Under my bed."

"Does anyone live there?" asked the Blimlim.

"I don't know. I'm afraid to look."

"You needn't be afraid if I'm there. Is it quiet?"

Anatole thought about this.

"I guess so. Grandma never cleans under the bed since she lost the mop."

"Did you say a mop?" exclaimed the Blimlim. "I found a mop not long ago."

"You did?"

"But I don't seem to remember where I put it," murmured the Blimlim nervously.

Silence fell, the silence of two friends who enjoy each other's company even when they are not conversing.

"When shall we leave?" asked Anatole at last.

"When your friends leave, we'll leave, too. Climb on my head."

The Blimlim streaked through the forest, its scales throwing sparks, and stopped behind the fountain of Venus, where the party of merrymakers thought they had just seen a rush of fireflies. In the twilight Anatole could make out the shadows of his friends: Thérèse's quick shadow, Gilles' drooping silhouette, and Madame d'Aulnoy's majestic shape, as large and elegant as a tree. They huddled around the ship as the Emperor of the Moon led the way on board, and their voices carried clearly.

"A pity about Frère Jacques," said Gilles. "He was a good-hearted fellow. I liked him."

"Perhaps the Blimlim has not eaten him," said Madame d'Aulnoy. "Perhaps he's found the golden bough."

And then Thérèse's voice: "How dark it is! Isn't it time to light the lamps?"

Lanterns twinkled at stem and stern. Even after the

ship sailed out of sight, Anatole, left behind on the dark shore, could hear the frail music of their laughter.

"They're gone," said the Blimlim with a sigh. "Do you know the way back to your country?"

"That way," said Anatole, and he pointed into the darkness.

"You are pointing to the end of the world," said the Blimlim. "If you're wrong, we will fall off the earth, and who knows what will become of us?"

"It may be the end of the world," said Anatole, "but that is where I live."

"Very well," said the Blimlim. "Hang on tight."

And it plunged into the black water and swam straight into the moonless night, with Anatole on its head. Its body cut the water like a skillfully guided blade, scarcely disturbing it, making no noise and no waves. Neither spoke for a long time.

Suddenly the Blimlim shuddered. "I say, look there. Do you see a tree?"

"Where?" cried Anatole.

"Just in front of us."

Anatole clapped his hands.

"That's our hatrack! That's Grandpa's cap and that's Jon's umbrella and there's Grandpa's old sweater hanging on it. We're nearly home. We're headed for the front hall."

To avoid a collision, the Blimlim passed behind the mirror and the telephone stand and sailed upstairs. Suddenly all its scales stood on end.

"Hark! I hear the clash of weapons. Are we in enemy waters?"

"The clash of weapons? Oh, that's our radiators turning on. Nothing to worry about. This is Grandma's dressing table."

They brushed his grandmother's perfume bottles and slipped behind the headboard of her bed, gliding behind Grandpa's bed and round the other side. The Blimlim sniffed his hand as it lay on the covers. Grandpa opened his eyes and waved as Anatole and the Blimlim blew across the hall.

Through the open door he saw his mother's dolls smiling at him from their high shelf and Jon asleep in the rocker beside the bed.

"Do you see that dark space there?" asked Anatole, pointing. "That's your house."

Swish! The Blimlim darted out of the wallpaper and disappeared under the bed, dropping Anatole head first into the blankets. His sneakers and his dump truck clattered to the floor.

"Aggggg," yawned Jon.

Anatole hung his head over the side of the bedclothes and whispered, "Blimlim! How do you like it?"

"Comfy," answered a voice thick with dust. "You're not scared any more, are you?"

"No," said Anatole.

"What a relief not to be guarding treasure! Wake me up if you need my help."

"Do you want anything to eat?"

"Eat!" exclaimed the Blimlim. "I'm much too old for such dependencies."

Jon stirred again. Anatole scooted under the covers

"Grandpa opened his eyes and waved as Anatole and the Blimlim blew across the hall."

and pretended to be asleep as Jon rubbed his eyes, scratched his back, gazed around him in bewilderment, and tiptoed out of the room.

Thump! Grandma's feet struck the floor. Anatole jumped out of bed. He could hear water running in the bathroom. Grandpa was sitting on the edge of the bathtub. Bzzzz! whined the electric razor as Grandma ran it over his cheek.

"Good morning," said Grandma. "Try to be quiet, will you? Jon fell asleep in his chair, and he's stiff as starch. He's gone back to bed."

Bzzz! sang the razor over Grandpa's chin.

"I saw Anatole this morning in the wallpaper," said Grandpa.

Grandma snapped off the razor and kissed his ear.

"Of all the nonsense I ever heard, that takes the cake. But, Anatole, guess what I found under the bathroom sink? My tea canister."

"Did you, Grandma?"

"And guess what else I found? Kneel down here and look."

Together they crouched under the sink. Grandma pointed to the place where the pipe joined the wall.

"A garden in the wallpaper," she exclaimed. "I never saw it before. Look, here's an apple tree and some yellow violets—"

"Those are marigolds, Grandma," said Anatole, "not violets."

His grandmother studied them.

"So they are," she agreed. "I wish I could pick some. I bet they'd smell nice."

"They don't smell at all," said Anatole. "They're made of topaz."

"Topaz, indeed," snorted Grandma. "How do you know they're made of topaz?"

"I touched them," said Anatole.